TIME'S UP:
PRIORITIZE YOURSELF NOW
Simple Self-Care for the Busy Days

AYANA THOMAS

Copyright © 2020 by Ayana Thomas

All rights reserved. No part of this publication may be reproduced, distributed, or transmitted in any form or by any means, including photocopying, recording, or other electronic or mechanical methods, without the prior written permission of the publisher, except in the case of brief quotations embodied in critical reviews and certain other noncommercial uses permitted by copyright law.

For permission requests and more information, write to the author at foryoulibertywrites@gmail.com.

Liberty Writes
Washington, DC
Printed in the United States of America

ISBN: 978-0-578-77509-8

COMMITMENT TO READERS

I want every word that I write to bring readers to a place of liberty – free from the concerns of this world, free from the cares of life, and free from self-destruction.

The bottom line is – I want you to be free.

The passion behind my work stems from experiences that have refined me. There is a famous saying that "experience is the best teacher." My perspective is that shared experience is the bridge to greatness. Equipped with the knowledge of shared experience, we can be strategic about the steps that we take to walk into our purpose. The same is true for you. By committing the time to read and work through Time's Up, you can be more strategic about caring for yourself and those you love.

Peace and Liberty!

Ayana

In my first book, *Life Light*, I introduced the reflection prompt and the **Liberty Writes 24 Second Rule**™. Although there are no reflection prompts in *Time's Up*, there is still the necessity for you to be familiar with reflective practice. Reflection helps you to be present with your past and present thoughts and feelings so that you can successfully navigate your steps forward.

Reflection Pro-Tip: At a minimum, use the reflection prompt to practice the **Liberty Writes 24 Second Rule**™. Close your eyes and take three deep breaths. This should take you about 24 seconds to complete. These deep breaths help to center you and give you a break from the racing thoughts in your mind. At some reflection prompts, that will be all that you need.

It is important for you to focus your thoughts and listen to your inner voice. Some thoughts might be intimidating initially. Do not let that deter you.

Happy Reflecting!

The Set Up

As I am typing this, there is no time in my schedule for me to write this book (do you see the irony...lol). If I do not get this done now, it will never be finished. Completing this book for mass consumption has been on my list of things to do now for months (literally). Back when things were "normal", my days were a constant juggling act. Wake up. Hit the door. Traffic. Work. Try to eat right. More work. Traffic again. Work. Helping People. Caring for my family. More work. Maybe exercise. Work. Everyone else in the house goes to sleep. Really work (because I can focus now). Squeeze in a few hours to sleep. Do it all over again – wake up, work...you get the drift.

The context for this book is so unique because I am finishing it in the midst of the global pandemic of 2020. It is possible that when it is published and when you read it, we will still be quarantined. It is also possible that when you read this book, 50 years will have passed and you may have no idea what I am talking about – but someone in your life will. Ask them about their pandemic experience.

Maybe it was my naïveté, but I definitely thought the pandemic would only last a few weeks. Especially if everyone stayed home and followed instructions. However, that is not the case. The pandemic rages on.

Honestly, pandemic days may be more complicated than "normal" days. The stressors created by the pandemic are unfathomable.

TIME'S UP: PRIORITIZE YOURSELF NOW

Staying inside for days at a time or taking a chance breathing free, regular outside air creates so much pent up stress, anxiety, and aggravation for many. No one is exempt. We are enduring this very stressful moment in time, in solidarity. Fingers crossed that this season will soon end!

Oddly enough, I am working harder in pandemic than I was back when things were normal. In pandemic, the days go a little something like this: Wake up. Zoom. Zoom. Zoom. Run late for a Zoom because I have to go to the bathroom OR try to eat something (the heavens clearly did not design pandemic business hours for you to be able to do both at the same time). Zoom. Zoom. Zoom. Care for my family. Handle a few time sensitive work things (because you cannot work and Zoom at the same time). Maybe exercise (I am doing better with this). Grab dinner. Everyone else in the house goes to sleep. Really work (because I can focus now). Squeeze in a few hours to sleep. Do it all over again – wake up, zoom, repeat the day before. I believe you get the picture! Pandemic days are never-ending and they all run together. My conclusion is that there is never enough time to get all of the things done that need to get done. This is the truth in my world.

You might live in a perfect world where you have mastered balance. Perhaps, you get the prescribed 8-10 hours of sleep each night. Good for you. It is also possible that you exercise every day and eat all of your meals in the correct portions. Great work! However, you made it this far into the book, so I doubt that ALL of these things to do are congruent for you. Am I right?

If I am right, Hey Friend! Welcome! You are in good company. You are among the Greats – the Living Legends that get up every day make amazing contributions and do their very best to care for themselves (and others) in a world of mounting priorities. You may not know me well, but we share the same plight and I am here to help you. We will take this journey together!

DISCIPLINE - WHO? WHERE? WHAT?

When it comes to discipline for the things that I need most, I find that it is better to have someone tell me what to do. This is certainly my truth – maybe not yours. In my areas of improvement, I believe in collaborating with experts, who tell me what to do and how to do it so that I can develop the skills necessary to do these things on my own. You know the whole, "teach a man to fish" concept. So in areas where I lack discipline (exercising, dieting, SELF-CARE, etc.), having experts tell me what to do, ensures that I get whatever IT is, done.

Consider this book a tool of accountability. Consider me your self-care accountability partner (insert hugs and lots of laughs). I do not have all of the answers, but I know that we need help. You. Me. Us. We. We need help. We need support creating a self-care strategy because if we could do it with the time, resources, and knowledge that we have, it would be done. Nevertheless, it is not. So here we are. Let's get into it.

WHO CAN RESIST A GOOD DARE? THE HISTORY OF THE LIBERTY WRITES SELF-CARE DARE 52™

I am assuming because you picked up this book, that you recognize how important it is to care for yourself. When I launched my business in 2019, I started networking in a way that I had never done before. These conversations gave me the opportunity to talk with people from all different walks of life. The common denominator in many of these conversations was that time was of the essence and that there was not enough time for self-care.

I was inspired to create the **Liberty Writes Self-Care Dare 52™** to help people develop intentionality around self-care. Essentially, I challenged men, women, and families around the world to join in on this challenge to prioritize self-care in some unique way each week.

Every week, for 52 weeks (a year for those that did not do well in math), I shared a self-care prompt and dared challengers to follow through and complete the dare.

The feedback from the challenge was overwhelmingly positive. Challengers regularly posted pictures from their self-care dare and commented on how useful the weekly prompts had become in helping them to silence the noise around them and focus on self- care. With all of the positive energy around the challenge, I decided to compile the weekly challenges into a book so that others can have the benefit of caring for themselves in a thoughtful and comprehensive way.

Doubling Down

Despite the fact that I have not spent any real time in casinos placing bets (blame my aversion to risk and lack of solid gambling teachers), I am familiar with the concept of doubling down. The term implies that you invest fully or strengthen your commitment to a particular strategy or course of action. In the case of self-care, there are no risks, per se. However, there is a necessity for you to make a commitment and to double down on that commitment, to see this through. Can I trust you to put yourself first each week? I hope so.

If you stray away or life gets too busy, just know that you can always come back and pick up where you left off. Judgement free. Stress free. All vibes of positivity ahead. I will be here with open arms – to encourage you to keep going.

Going forward, I am going to say less and trust you to take the next steps on your own, with guidance from the book, of course. *Time's Up* contains 52 self-care dare prompts. The expectation however, is that you concentrate on self-care by completing at least one Dare/Challenge each week. Do not feel pressured to commit to more than one dare on a weekly basis.

 This is a no stress, no judgement zone! There is no grade book and there is no right way to complete each dare. Do it your way! The dare is intended to bring you some sense of peace, joy, or just good ole fun. It is an opportunity to put everything in your life on pause (sometimes for just a few minutes) to take your mind off things and focus on you.

Each dare will give you a general idea of what is expected and then some steps or information that will aid you in completing the dare. Some dares will be easier than other dares. On light weeks, give yourself a break. If you are feeling like you need more, find a simple "off the books" way to care for yourself in addition to your weekly challenge. Some dares will require that you make a plan or allocate resources (money, time, etc.) to get it done. There is always space for creative interpretation and doing what feels right for you.

Thank you so much for making this commitment to take care of yourself. Your commitment to self-care means the world to me and I am hopeful that as you work through the book, that it will come to mean the world to you!

For Your Consideration
A FEW RANDOM THOUGHTS

If you are anything like me, you want all of the answers up front without having to read the instructions. I totally understand. This section provides you some additional "rules" that can help you to have a more meaningful self-care experience. They may or may not be applicable to you.

Check Out the Reference Section

Being the teacher that I am, I thought it was helpful to provide additional resources to aid your understanding or to help you think broader about certain dares. In these cases, there is a reference at the end of the dare description to remind you to look for the cool article links at the back of the book. If for some reason, technology progresses (similar to what we see in the movie Minority Report) and people are still reading this book hundreds of years later, find the closest thing to Google and run a quick search for dare topic related information.

Plan Time in to Complete Your Dare

This is important. Everything I do in life is on my calendar. Add the self-care dare to your calendar, as a reminder to complete the dare on a weekly basis. If you know that weekends are better for self-care, pencil it in. If there is a day of the week that you are commitment free regularly, pencil self-care in. Whenever you complete the dare, you have to plan to make sure that it gets done. Complete the dare at a time that will be most beneficial for you!

Family Challengers

If you are a parent or caregiver, it is very possible that you will need to complete each dare alone to give yourself space to love on you. I also know that it can be hard to break away from the family sometimes. Use your best discretion and ultimately do what is best for you.

You can invite your family and friends to complete the weekly challenge with you (encourage them to buy *Time's Up* or gift it to them). At various points throughout the book, I have included instructions for Family Challengers. These additional instructions help you to turn the dare for you, into a dare for everyone. Completing the dare as a family can be a great way to bring your loved ones together and be present with each other.

Milestone Weeks

Putting yourself first for a whole year can seem daunting and it can be even more difficult to commit to as time goes on. Dare weeks 10, 26, and 52 are set aside as milestone weeks. These milestones help you to celebrate your progress over the year. I am only noting this here, in the event that you decide to complete any of the weekly dares out of sequence and you stumble upon the milestone weeks.

Finally, Connect to the Bigger Picture

I mentioned earlier that there were amazing people all over the world that completed the **Liberty Writes Self-Care Dare 52**™. Consider yourself part of the greater self-care community. If you would like to check in with others and see what others are doing, you can take the following steps:

- Follow @foryoulibertywrites on Instagram

- Take a video, a picture, or simply post that you have completed the Self-Care Dare. Please use the hashtag #selfcaredare52 and please tag Liberty Writes in your post. Through the hashtag, you will be able to see other brave Challengers (past and present) working through their weekly dare.

Welcome to the Self-Care Dare

Dance to Your Favorite Song

I dare you to crank the volume up and dance to your favorite song! Dance like there is no one watching!

Practice Smiling

This week, we smile! I dare you to practice smiling. Yes, smile long, smile hard, and smile often. Smile for all of the good reasons! Smile when you get upset. Smile when you are frustrated. As soon as you encounter negative vibes, greet them with a smile. Smile to brighten your day!

 CHECK THE REFERENCE SECTION – There are a number of scientific ways that smiling improves your overall well-being.

 FAMILY CHALLENGERS – I dare your whole family to smile! Share this challenge with your family. I am willing to bet that a smiling family will change the vibe of the house.
Thank me later!

Dare

7 Days – 7 Amazing Ways

I dare you to say something amazing to yourself every day. For 7 days, we will practice self-affirmation. This is a simple way to love on yourself quickly and completely stress free. You can complete the dare in the morning when you are getting ready for the day. The dare can be a reminder when you hit a rough spot in the day. You can also wait until the end of the day, when you are quieting yourself before bed and use it as a reminder of your bossness.

Whichever time works best for you, be intentional about making time to affirm your greatness. 7 days, 7 amazing ways!

Dare

Turn Your Phone Off for One Hour

I dare you to turn your phone off for one hour. Power your phone off. When our phones start acting up, what do we do? We turn them off to give them an opportunity to reset. We are glued to our phones constantly for everything. We do not realize how the phone has the ability to influence our mood, our productivity, and our overall progress. So turn it off and give yourself the same opportunity to reset.

Be sure to notify the necessary friends and family members that you will be away from your phone for an hour. Once you have disconnected enough to feel comfortable turning the phone off, start the clock for 60 minutes (obviously the mental clock because your phone will be off). During this time, no email and I want to say no tv, but if you need tv to relax go ahead. Try to focus on nothing. If you feel your thoughts drifting to your plans for the upcoming week or work that needs to be done around the house, reel them back in and focus on nothing.

Suggestions for your hour of no phone:

- Sit still with no stimulation
- Take a nap
- Go for a walk
- Read a book
- Sit outside in the fresh air
- Take a bath

 FAMILY CHALLENGERS - everyone's phone should be off at the same time - use this time to be present with family members. Play games, read, or share family stories together.

Pick any 5-minute interval and take a walk outside

I dare you to take a walk outside. You can select any 5-minute interval for your walk (5 minutes, 10 minutes, 15 minutes, etc.).

The catch is that the walk does not count if you are walking to a specific location. I walk outside every day to get to meetings. The reality though, is that these walks are not peaceful – and they are definitely not an intentional form a self-care. While I am walking, I am constantly thinking about my destination and what I have to do when I arrive. Walks like this do not count.

Take a break from life this week - even if it is only for 5 minutes and take a walk. No headphones or airpods. Be present with yourself and with your surroundings.

 FAMILY CHALLENGERS - Take a walk together. Let the kid(s) decide on how long the walk will be. Challenge them to select a 5 minutes interval.

TIME'S UP: PRIORITIZE YOURSELF NOW

Dare

Treat yourself to something under $10

AYANA THOMAS

I dare you to treat yourself to something special. Your treat cannot be more than $10. Tap into your creativity and find a way to reward yourself for all of your hard work and amazingness!

PS. If you drink the same cup of $6.89 coffee every day, that does not qualify as a treat. Do something different, step out of your comfort zone and see what you can do to add happiness to your life with only $10.

Celebrate Last Week's Accomplishments
(8 of them)

I dare you to reflect on the past week and celebrate eight accomplishments you had in the week. The accomplishments could be big or small - whatever mattered most to you. For example, folding the big pile of laundry that had been sitting on the couch for weeks could have been an accomplishment. Similarly, taking a big exam or getting a promotion could have also been accomplishments for you. You make the list - your way. Find eight wins!

If you have time to do some additional reflecting, think about what you would like to accomplish in the coming week. Take a few notes and then see it through.

Dare

The Gift of Affirmation

This week, I dare you to give someone the gift of affirmation. Self-affirmation is empowering and healing. Imagine sharing that positive energy with someone else. You'd be surprised how much affirming others can also boost your vibe.

Here's the deal - CALL someone (facetime or regular call) that you care about and start the conversation with this prompt: "can you give me 60 seconds to celebrate you"? When they say yes, spend 60 uninterrupted seconds (or 1 minute) telling them why they are amazing, why they matter, why you care for them. Make a few notes before you call them if that will help you.

Affirmation of self and others matters. Use your self-care dare time this week to spread love. In reality, affirming others will be equally, if not more, rewarding for you.

 **CHECK THE REFERENCE SECTION**

Dare 9

Focus on the Good Life

I dare you to focus on the good in your life by creating a "good jar". Get a cup - a red dixie cup or something similar is fine (don't make this complicated - ok friends). All week focus on the good things in your life. Be intentional about this.

At a minimum write down two things to put in your cup each day. By the end of the week, you should have at least 14 good things that you can pull from as a reminder when you might be facing a tough time in the future - thank me later!

It is true that the bad stuff in life sucks, but the good will always outweigh the bad! Keep your GOOD jar around to keep the good thoughts top of mind. In the past, I have also created a faith and answered prayer jar. Being able to see these jars fill up over time is a great way to build confidence in different areas of your life.

 FAMILY CHALLENGERS - Encourage members of your family to create a GOOD jar. This will help everyone in the family to develop greater perspective and appreciation for the GOODness of life!

TIME'S UP: PRIORITIZE YOURSELF NOW

Self-Care DIY

YOU MADE IT TO WEEK 10 in the self-care dare. Congratulations on reaching this milestone! For 10 weeks, two months, and a little over 60 days, you have been making the time to prioritize and be present with yourself. Kudos to you!

This week I dare you, to self-care Do It Yourself (DIY). Do the thing that you love most to take care of yourself. Remember to keep your self-care dare simple and achievable - do not create unnecessary stress by overthinking.

If you cannot think of a challenge, please repeat a dare from weeks 1-9.

We have 10 weeks of consistent self-care under our belt and we have many weeks ahead! Take care of yourself!

TIME'S UP: PRIORITIZE YOURSELF NOW

Dwell Among The Clouds

I dare you to dwell among the clouds. Spend some time this week admiring the clouds. Cloud watching relieves stress, intensifies focus, and heightens mindfulness.

Be intentional about reflecting on the form, pattern, and flow of the clouds in the sky. Make this commitment for at least five minutes at some point this week. If it is warm enough where you are to step outside for a few minutes, take in some fresh air during your time of reflection.

 FAMILY CHALLENGERS - This is a great exercise to share as a family. Hearing others perspective about what they see is eye opening!

 **CHECK THE REFERENCE SECTION**

Dare

Stretch It Out

I dare you to stretch yourself - literally and figuratively. It is important that you are always thinking of what is next for you. Your next could be next week, next month, or next year. In either case, it is good to be forward thinking. There is no point in waiting until January 1st to make a plan for the year. As we have seen in 2020, a few days could completely change the trajectory of the year.

Spend some time before getting into bed or when you get out of bed stretching. Additionally, this week think about ways that you can create stretch assignments for yourself. What are things that you can do to stretch outside of your comfort zone? Maybe you start writing your business plan. Or maybe you dust off your resume and start looking for new jobs. Or maybe you try a new exercise you have been hesitant to try. Whatever you do, stretch yourself.

 **CHECK THE REFERENCE SECTION**

Dare

Sing A Song

This week, I dare you to sing a song. Find a song that motivates you, inspires you, affirms you, or encourages you. Lock yourself in the bathroom and belt the song out in the mirror or sit and mediate to it. Take this 3-5 minutes for yourself. Listen to the words of the song and let them move you.

Dare 14

Declutter A Space

A cluttered life, is a _____ life. There are so many ways to fill in that blank. Clutter could be a major distraction for you. Clutter could be keeping you from reaching your peak potential. Clutter could also be the reason you are procrastinating taking action on something important in your life. Over the next three weeks, our focus will be on decluttering a different area of our lives.

This week, I dare you to declutter a space. Start small - pick a cabinet, drawer, or closet at home or at work that needs to be cleaned out. Do not overcomplicate this. Set your timer for 45 minutes and do not spend more time than that. If you know up front, that cleaning out and organizing a space will take more than 45 minutes, pick something else to focus on.

 **CHECK THE REFERENCE SECTION**

TIME'S UP: PRIORITIZE YOURSELF NOW

Declutter Electronically

Cleaning out can be rewarding for so many reasons – there are definitely visual, physical, and psychological rewards. So let's keep the party going.

This week, I challenge you to declutter electronically. Clean out your email. UNSUBSCRIBE from promo ads and other junk mail vibes that are cluttering up your inbox. Unfollow pages on social media that do not feed you messages of positivity or prosperity. Finally, CANCEL unnecessary subscriptions for services that you are not regularly utilizing.

Let's continue the work of cleaning up and clearing out, to reach a new level of clarity and perspective.

Dare 16

Declutter Your Mind

I would say that we are closer to living a clutter-free life. However, many of us have quite a bit of clutter to deal with and these baby steps the last two weeks have been just that...baby steps. By now at least, you should have one clean closet/drawer/space and you should have less junk accumulating electronically. Big ups to you!

This week, I dare you to declutter your mind. Find 15-20 minutes to do a quick brain dump. Here is what you need to do...

- Make a list of all of the things on your mind (List 1). Take no more than 5 minutes to complete List 1.

- From List 1, **circle** the things you can resolve quickly and on your own (List 2). **Star** the things that are long-term and/or will require you to ask someone else to help (List 3).

- Knock out the things on List 2 that you can do right away.

- Make a plan for the items on list 3 - not necessarily now but in the near future since you have identified your long term priorities

My hope is that this exercise will help you to be present (mind and body).

*If you have *Life Light: The Workbook*, I would like to direct you to the Present and Accounted Exercise.*

Dare

Take Flight

AYANA THOMAS

Spend a few minutes looking for planes in the sky. Try not to get frustrated. Spend a moment in a space of stillness – while you focus on the blessings in the sky. Make a mental note of the amazing things you see, even if you do not see any planes.

TIME'S UP: PRIORITIZE YOURSELF NOW

Do Not Disturb

Normally, my phone sets for DND at 10pm every night. That automatic setting protects my rest from late night phone calls, texts messages, or unwanted alerts. This is important because the slightest sound or mental stimulation can throw off my sleeping pattern and have me lying awake at night - thinking and wasting good rest time.

During a recent holiday, I put my phone on do not disturb during the day. Do Not Disturb - during the day (big wow)! Game changer! I did not realize how frequently throughout the day I was being distracted by alerts or notifications. All of my emergency contacts were able to get through and I still checked my phone periodically to make sure tragedy did not strike. However, making time to put my phone on DND was so helpful to my daily restoration and productivity. It also eased some of my anxiety around connecting with people.

This week, I dare you to find some DND time. Maybe you have a project that requires your concentration. Or you need an hour to read quietly (I recommend *Life Light*). Or maybe you just need to sit still. Put your phone on DND and watch that uninterrupted time work to your advantage.

Quick Note: I want to clarify that DND is different from silent. If you still receive vibrating alerts to your phone on silent - then you need to take it a step further and disable alerts on the phone altogether for a short time. DND is the perfect fix.

Dare

Please, Be Still!

I dare you to Be Still. Find a few moments throughout the week, to just be still. It's very simple. Sit still. No TV, no phone, no people, and no stimulation - just you in this present moment. Focus on your breathing. Focus on settling your mind. Sit for just a few minutes or as long as you need to conquer the week!

 **CHECK THE REFERENCE SECTION**

Dare 20

Color Me Happy

I dare you to break out the crayons and the colored pencils and color yourself happy. Drawing, sketching, or even just writing your thoughts out is scientifically proven to reduce stress and anxiety. Do not put unnecessary pressure on yourself to produce a perfect product. Just draw what you see and feel. Take a few moments this week to color yourself happy!

 **CHECK THE REFERENCE SECTION**

TIME'S UP: PRIORITIZE YOURSELF NOW

Move Your Body

I dare you to move your body. Make some time this week to get up and move around. We do a lot of sitting - at work, at home, and in other places. Do something different this week. Try a new dance class or exercise class. Play a game of flag football or soccer. Turn on your favorite album and dance around the house. Whatever you do, get up and move.

Hopefully, the weather will be nice enough where you are able to move around outside. If not, indoor movement will work just fine.

TIME'S UP: PRIORITIZE YOURSELF NOW

Love List

This week I challenge you to create a Love List. That's right.

Spend the next 7 days focusing your energy on loving on YOU. Here is how you do it...

1. Identify 7 things that you love about yourself (no more than 2 physical attributes). You can write down all 7 things on your love list at the beginning of the week or you can build on your list throughout the week.

2. Pick two times throughout the day and set an alarm or reminder. When your reminder goes off, confess your love focus for that day. You can sing to yourself, dance to yourself, or just tell yourself (OUTLOUD) what you are in love with about YOU!

By the end of the week, you should have an awesome list of positive affirmations to remind you of why you are so deserving of love.

Dare

Play Around

I dare you to play around a little. I know it may sound silly, but from a psychological perspective, play is encouraged for stress relief in adults. For you, play may consist of pulling out an old board game, trying to master a Rubik's Cube, or building a lego fortress by yourself or with someone you love.

Try to carve out 30 mins to an hour this week for play. Phone apps, online games, and video games do not count. Take a break from the screen and do something with your hands. Go outside for a game of kickball (assuming the weather where you are permits). Do something to break up the patterns in your life, free your mind, and engage your body differently!

 **CHECK THE REFERENCE SECTION**

Dare

Change it Up

Change something minor this week and see what difference it makes. Rearrange furniture. Change your walking routine. Take a different path to work. Eat something different for breakfast or lunch. The change could be disorienting, but it could also be amazing. Be bold!

Dare

KidNAP Yourself

This week, I dare you to slow yourself down and take a nap. Listen to your body and rest. Naps can give you the boost that you need to get through the rest of the day or a difficult moment. Select a 15-minute interval and close your eyes.

Dare 26

Celebrate Yourself

There is excited energy from the author's pen this week. Why??? You made it to dare 26 of our 52-week self-care dare. That means we made it through a whole six months of being intentional about loving on ourselves, prioritizing ourselves, and making space for ourselves (and our loved ones). I hope this journey has been beneficial for you.

This week, I dare you to celebrate yourself and your wins. Take a moment to write down 3-5 things you have done well... this year, this week, or even just today. Without worrying about what you did not do right or agonizing over how you may have failed in the process, **just focus on the win - big or small**.

Do something simple that feels like celebration to you - watch a movie, have a glass of wine, call a friend, treat yourself to something nice. You get the drift. Celebrate!

TIME'S UP: PRIORITIZE YOURSELF NOW

Smell – O – Rama

I dare you to surround yourself with pleasant scents. Make time for a little aromatherapy. If you have a thing for candles, take a stroll through the nearest candle store. Pick out a new scent to energize your home. Not up for a walk on the wild side? Stick to the normal scents that make you feel most comfortable.

If candles do not do it for you, consider purchasing an oil diffuser and picking up some essential oils to liven up your home and mood.

TIME'S UP: PRIORITIZE YOURSELF NOW

Meditation Moment

This week, I dare you to make time for meditation. There are so many ways to meditate. Part of this dare, is to find the method of meditation that works for you. If you do not already meditate on a regular basis, I encourage you to spend at least 15 minutes researching meditation methods to find a suitable option for you. Also, consider researching apps that offer guided meditations and other meditation resources. Spend some time meditating this week. Meditate at a short interval that works best for you.

Dare 29

Spice It Up

This week I dare you, spice it up. I will leave this dare up to your interpretation. Spicing it up, could be literal for you. It could mean that you add some new spices to your favorite meal or beverage. Spicing it up could mean that you wear a new dress or pair of tennis shoes that make you feel sexy. Spice it up safely and with self-care in mind.

Dare 30

Do Some Smoothie Soothing

This week, I dare you to enjoy a delicious smoothie. Smoothies are a great blend of goodness. Smoothies have all of your favorite ingredients mixed in together – producing a healthy and nutritious outcome. Smoothies can be soothing in all seasons of the year. Whether you DIY your smoothie or go to the nearest smoothie shop, make time to enjoy this treat.

Swap option – if you hate smoothies, you can sub in the beverage of your choice.

Dare

How You Doin?

This week, I dare you to text 5 of your family or friends that you have not spoken to in a while and inquire about their wellbeing. There is great comfort in knowing that the people that you love are well! Do not leave anyone on read – respond to the text messages and let your loved ones know how you are doing as well.

TIME'S UP: PRIORITIZE YOURSELF NOW

Do Nothing

In some cases doing nothing is the best thing you can do. It is ok. Rest is productive. Listen to your inner-voice and pay attention to the signs your body is sending to you. Do nothing for a minimum of 10 minutes.

 FAMILY CHALLENGERS - Have everyone in the family take a moment to do nothing. This might be extremely challenging for younger members of your family, but model the expectation for little ones to be still (as long as they can).

Dare 33

Water Ways

This week, I dare you to drink 8 cups of water each day. Yes, you will make many trips to the bathroom. Consider it a cleansing. Water consumption has so many amazing benefits for your overall health. Make a checklist or find an app that will help you track your water intake.

TIME'S UP: PRIORITIZE YOURSELF NOW

Feel It In The Air

AYANA THOMAS

This week, I dare you to take a few minutes to step out and get some fresh air. No airpods – no distractions. Stay outside for at least 7 minutes. If the weather is pleasant, stay outside as long as you can.

Dare 35

Say What Now?

This week, I dare you to spend some time talking to yourself. Honestly, you are the best conversationalist. You know you better than anyone else does. Talking to yourself outloud can help you to prioritize your thoughts or to visualize what you have been thinking about. As an introvert, I often have conversations with myself to prepare for conversations that I anticipate will be confrontational or difficult in the future. These conversations help me to reduce anxiety about the conversation.

You are not crazy if you talk to yourself. You know what you need. You know what boosts your confidence. Say it to yourself loud and proud!

TIME'S UP: PRIORITIZE YOURSELF NOW

Lead with Laughter

I dare you to laugh every day. Laughter is good for the soul and is contagious. Laughter releases endorphins and makes you feel better, even in a bad situation. Keep it simple. Do not overthink it. Set a timer and spend 30 seconds laughing each day.

Dare

37

My Treat

AYANA THOMAS

This week, I dare you to give/send someone $10 for lunch. You can also pay it forward by paying for someone's meal or beverage in line after you. Giving makes room for more!

Dare

38

Stay and Play

I dare you to plan a staycation. You may not be able to travel to a remote island or your favorite vacation destination, but you certainly can be creative with your staycation. Even if you only "go away" for the evening or a few hours, stay present in the moment. Relax your mind and enjoy your surroundings!

TIME'S UP: PRIORITIZE YOURSELF NOW

Dare

Step Outside

Sometimes we need a shift in our perspective to heighten awareness and in some cases enhance gratefulness. I dare you to take a step outside for just 2 minutes. Pay attention to your senses. Do not be afraid to be reflective. Welcome what comes to you in this moment.

What did you see?

What did you hear?

What did you feel?

What do you need in this moment?

Dare

Say It Like You Mean It

This week, I dare you to say it, like you mean it. Find time to affirm yourself this week. Below, I have included four easy prompts. All you have to do is finish the prompt with a positive thought.

- I am....
- I can...
- I will...
- I have...

Dare 41

Watch It Unfold

There is nothing like a good tv show or movie. You worked hard this week! I dare you to make time to unwind to your favorite TV show or movie. I am not suggesting that you binge watch an entire series, but two or three episodes will not hurt you. Enjoy!

Dare 42

I Spy With My Two Eyes

This week, I dare you to take a walk around the corner (at home or at work). Play a quick game of I Spy.

- Do you see something green?
- Do you see something breathing?
- Do you see something that inspires peace?
- Do you see something that makes you smile?
- Do you see something unique?

TIME'S UP: PRIORITIZE YOURSELF NOW

Musical Chairs

AYANA THOMAS

This week, I dare you to sit somewhere different at least three days this week. If you always sit in the same chair at the dinner table, pick another seat. If you always drive, consider letting someone else drive you or taking an uber to your destination. Having trouble connecting with members of your family, find a seat in their space. You would be surprised how something as simple as sitting somewhere else can help you to see differently and create new synergies for yourself and others.

TIME'S UP: PRIORITIZE YOURSELF NOW

Dare

44

4 The Easy Way

This week, I dare you to give yourself permission to rest, heal, change, and love. Find a way to be intentional about focusing on each of these areas this week. Take some notes, if that will help you to be thoughtful. The time is yours. Take the time you need.

TIME'S UP: PRIORITIZE YOURSELF NOW

Dare

Let It Go

You stress less when you stop trying to control things that you cannot control. This week, I dare you to go with the flow. This can be hard for some, but I have confidence that you can relax and let things free flow. Check in at the end of the week with yourself to assess how well you have done. If you did a great job, celebrate. If you failed miserably, try again.

TIME'S UP: PRIORITIZE YOURSELF NOW

Apply The Pressure

Applying pressure to your pressure points increases mindfulness and reduces stress. I dare you to spend five minutes massaging your pressure points.

 **CHECK THE REFERENCE SECTION**

TIME'S UP: PRIORITIZE YOURSELF NOW

Keep It Real

This week, I dare you to check-in. Reality checks are so critical to life. Stay objective and stay in the now. Grab a piece of paper and write yourself a note. How are you doing? What is happening around that you cannot control? What can you control? What are you doing that is preventing you from moving forward? How can you overcome these obstacles?

Set 10 minutes aside to check-in with yourself.

Dare 48

Back At It Again – DND

This week, I dare you to find a time to put your phone on Do Not Disturb. We have done this before. You are not new to this, you are true to this. Temporarily free yourself from unnecessary distractions. Repurpose this time to do something that helps you get closer to reaching a personal goal this week.

Dare

Be SMART

Keep it simple, but create a SMART self-care goal for the week. You can do it. You are a self-care guru at this point. I believe in you.

Learning how to create a SMART goal strategy will help you to continue your self-care journey when you've completed the book.

SMART Goals Are:

- Specific

- Measurable

- Achievable

- Relevant

- Timebound

A SMART self-care goal could be: I will go running two days, for 15 minutes before Wednesday.

Dare 50

Think Happy Thoughts

I dare you to make a list of 20 things that make you happy. Set your phone timer for three minutes and make your list in rapid fire action. If you have a touch of OCD (like me), neatly number your paper before you start rattling off your happy thoughts. Keep your list to refer back to when the week gets difficult and you need to reframe your thoughts.

 FAMILY CHALLENGERS – Set the timer for five minutes and invite your family to join you in creating your list of happy thoughts.

Dare 51

Enjoy Something Sweet

This week, I dare you to find a sweet treat. Find a gourmet cupcake or pastry shop and make a moment to enjoy a guilt-free, treat. If you are sensitive to sugar, find a sugar free treat that meets your fancy.

Dare

Liberty Writes 24 Second Rule™

Kudos to You! You made it to the end of the road. You are to be commended for getting to this point in the journey.

This week, I encourage you to breathe in all of the good things. Take a moment this week, at least once, to practice the **Liberty Writes 24 Second Rule**™. Find 24 seconds and take three deep breaths in and out. Just breathe!

In Closing...

Clarity (from *Life Light: The Pursuit of your Best Self*)

Oh to be clear – to be seen clearly, to be heard clearly, and to see clearly. Clarity has two primary definitions: 1) to be coherent and intelligible and 2) to be transparent. When I think about clarity, I think about how uncomfortable it can be driving through a patch of fog. When you cannot see where you are going, your body has so many different reactions. As soon as the fog breaks, all of the anxiety and angst eases. Wouldn't it be nice if all of our days were totally clear?

Unfortunately, the way life works, we know that there will be cloudy days and days where the fog is so thick, that we don't feel like we can move forward. Some of us may even get stuck in this place for more than a few days, because we cannot function in the absence of clarity. I hope that *Life Light* has helped you develop a greater sense of clarity on the various topics included in the book. I hope that if you don't have clarity that you will do the work necessary to gain clarity – so that you can be fully present with yourself, others and the around. I also hope that you are able to use the strategies provided in this book to clear out the things in your life that may prevent you being able to see your purpose in a transparent way – no fog.

Every year, I complete a clarity cleanse to help me prepare for the year to come. It is a seven day cleanse that forces me to withdraw myself from life's unnecessary distractions (namely social media and

Netflix binge watching), so that I can seek direction. Sometimes the circumstances of life will not allow you to physically separate yourself from home or work to get the direction that you need in life. The clarity cleanse is designed to help you tap into your divine source to obtain guidance that helps you reach towards your greatness. The clarity cleanse helps you to focus on reflection - asking yourself the tough questions and dealing with the tough realities. More importantly, the clarity cleanse will help you come to solutions that will help you to walk clearly towards your future.

I hope that you are clear on my intentions for you to reach your highest potential. More importantly, it is my hope that you succeed there. Be open to evolution and follow peace with every step.

Details for the **Liberty Writes Clarity Cleanse** are included in *Life Light: The Workbook*.

REFERENCES

Dare 2: Practice Smiling

- https://www.verywellmind.com/top-reasons-to-smile- every-day-2223755

Dare 8: The Gift of Affirmation

- https://www.thedailypositive.com/10-statements- everyone-needs-hear/
- https://www.psychologytoday.com/us/blog/smart-relationships/201403/affirmations-the-why-what-how- and-what-if
- https://www.huffpost.com/entry/affirmations_b_3527028

Dare 11: Dwell Among The Clouds

- https://www.mentalfloss.com/article/75190/15-billowing- facts-about-cloudscts About Clouds
- https://www.stevespanglerscience.com/2014/08/20/beaut y-clouds/

Dare 12: Stretch It Out

- https://healthprep.com/living-healthy/health-benefits-of- stretching/?utm_source=bing&utm_medium=search&utm_campaign=267708539&utm_content=1275433808163758&utm_term=benefits%20of%20stretching&msclkid=31ff38fc23eb12afb5b26524ac11cb34
- https://www.verywellfit.com/stretching-101-2696342
- https://www.youtube.com/watch?v=eOWJsw_ARB0

REFERENCES

Dare 14 – Declutter A Space

- https://www.psychologytoday.com/us/blog/in- practice/201802/6-benefits-uncluttered-space

- https://tinybuddha.com/blog/7-ways-decluttered-life-can- result-decluttered-mind/

- https://www.glad.com/teachable-trash/tips-for- decluttering-your-home/?msclkid=08259d9e417b1c35b547c075846237d0 &utm_source=bing&utm_medium=cpc&utm_campaign=GLT_Generic_Teachable_Trash_Declutter_Phrase&utm_term=declutter&utm_content=Declutter_General&gclid=CJbR7oPto-YCFVPkswodKs0MNw&gclsrc=ds

Dare 19 – Be Still

- https://www.huffpost.com/entry/silence-brain-benefits_n_56d83967e4b0000de4037004

- https://makedapennycooke.com/practicing-stillness/

- https://unfoldyourfreedom.com.au/benefits-of-stillness/

Dare 20 – Color Me Happy

- https://www.colorit.com/blogs/news/85320388-amazing- benefits-of-coloring-for-adults

- https://www.cnn.com/2016/01/06/health/adult-coloring- books-popularity-mental-health/index.html

- https://www.developgoodhabits.com/benefits-adult- coloring/

REFERENCES

Dare 23 – Play Around

- https://www.helpguide.org/articles/mental- health/benefits-of-play-for-adults.htm
- https://www.verywellmind.com/stress-management-the-importance-of-fun-3144588
- https://www.nbcnews.com/better/health/adults-need- recess-too-here-s-why-you-should-make-ncna887396

Dare 46 – Apply The Pressure

- https://www.healthline.com/health/pain-relief/how-to- massage-your-pressure-points

Meet the Author

Readers all over the world are pursuing powered living with the literary works of Ayana Thomas. Ayana is committed to creating content that makes personal and professional development desirable and dynamic for everyone.

For upcoming appearances and books, visit ayanathomas.com.

**BUILDING PEOPLE
PURSUING POWERED LIVING**

LIBERTY WRITES IS HERE TO HELP YOU!

Liberty Writes is a people development brand that focuses on building the whole person. The brand offers career, family, and organizational development services.

Visit ayanathomas.com to learn more about our services!

www.ingramcontent.com/pod-product-compliance
Lightning Source LLC
Chambersburg PA
CBHW071405290426
44108CB00014B/1691